---❖---

"Pictures just come to my mind,
and then I tell my heart to go ahead."

Horace Pippin

_____

KITAGAWA UTAMARO. *Untitled*. Late 1790s. Woodblock, 14 ⁵/₁₆″ x 9 ¹¹/₁₆″.
Bayly Art Museum of the University of Virginia, Charlottesville.

COME
LOOK WITH ME

World of Play

Gladys S. Blizzard

THOMASSON-GRANT
Charlottesville, Virginia

This book is dedicated to my husband for his
steadfast backing of all my endeavors.

Published by Thomasson-Grant, Inc.
Designed by Lisa Lytton-Smith
Edited by Rebecca Beall Barns

99 98 97 96 95 94 93   5 4 3 2 1

Any inquiries should be directed to Thomasson-Grant, Inc.
One Morton Drive, Suite 500
Charlottesville, Virginia 22903-6806
(804) 977-1780

Library of Congress
Cataloging-in-Publication Data
Blizzard, Gladys S.
    Come look with me: world of play / Gladys S. Blizzard.
       p.   cm.
    Summary: Presents twelve works of art featuring people at play
accompanied by information about the artists, their styles, and the
techniques displayed in each work. Includes questions to stimulate
discussion.
    ISBN 1-56566-031-5
    1. Games in art – Juvenile literature. 2. Art appreciation – Juvenile
literature.   [1. Art appreciation. 2. Games in art.]
I. Title.
N8217.G34B65 1993
701'.1 – dc20   92–36263
                                                            CIP
                                                            AC

THOMASSON-GRANT

Contents

Preface 6

Introduction: How to use this book 7

Artist unknown, *Bull-Vaulting Fresco* 8

Attributed to Qasim Ibn Ali,
Shah-nameh: Siyavush Plays Polo Before Afrasiyab 10

Pieter Bruegel the Elder, *Children's Games* 12

Kitagawa Utamaro, *Untitled* 14

Jean-Siméon Chardin, *The House of Cards* 16

George Catlin, *Archery of the Mandan* 18

Winslow Homer, *Snap the Whip* 20

Maurice Prendergast, *The East River* 22

Horace Pippin, *Domino Players* 24

Diego Rivera, *Piñata* 26

Elaine de Kooning, *Baseball Players* 28

Red Grooms, *Fast Break* 30

Preface

For adults and children throughout the world, games and sports have always provided relaxation and amusement. They also challenge us, help us to develop mental and physical skills, and teach important social skills as well.

Each culture has portrayed its pastimes in art. Some games are unique to a time or place, but many are still widely played in a similar version today. Whatever the period or style, the way artists depict this subject in their work reflects something of what life was like in their time.

The intent of this book is to help stimulate children to look thoughtfully at works of art and to encourage them to share their thoughts about what they see. It was a challenge to select twelve works for this book that would present a variety of styles, techniques, and artists. Many friends and colleagues were called upon to help, so many that it is difficult to single out a few. Nevertheless, my editor, Rebecca Beall Barns, must be acknowledged for her interest, assistance, and guidance in this project.

How to use this book

COME LOOK WITH ME: WORLD OF PLAY is the fourth in a series of interactive art appreciation books for children. The first three books featured works of art with children, landscapes, and animals, respectively, as their subjects. This one features paintings, prints, and sculpture on the theme of people at play.

Like the first three, this book can be shared with one child or a small group of children. Each of the twelve works of art is paired with questions meant to stimulate thoughtful discussion between adults and children. The accompanying text gives some helpful background on each artist and his or her work of art. This can be read to the children or paraphrased for them while they are looking at the illustrations.

Ask a child to point to part of the painting while he or she talks about it. When working with a group, always ask if anyone has a different idea. There are no right or wrong answers to these questions, and everyone can benefit from the different perspectives that age, experience, and personal taste can bring to a group discussion. Limiting each session to a discussion of two or three works will help keep the interaction lively.

This book can be used at home, in classrooms, and in museums. There is no substitute for a visit to a museum to experience firsthand the color and texture of an artist's brush strokes and to see the size of the original work, but the methods used here can help teach children a way of looking at art and encourage them to share their understanding with others.

ARTIST UNKNOWN. *Bull-Vaulting Fresco.* c. 1500 B.C. Herakleion Museum, Crete. Scala/Art Resource, New York.

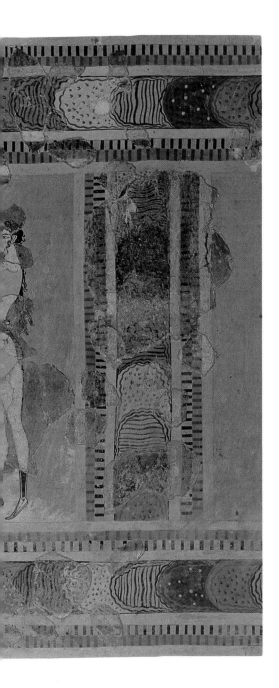

The bull and the people seem to be floating in space. What do you think the artist did to make them look that way?

Describe the different ways the artist showed movement.

Find a graceful, flowing line and trace it with your finger.

Which person seems to be in the most dangerous position? Why? What do you think will happen next?

A long time ago on the island of Crete in the Mediterranean Sea, people called Minoans decorated the walls of buildings with paintings noted for their playfulness and fluid lines. To make these paintings, called frescoes, the artists put layers of plaster on a wall to create a smooth surface, then painted on the last layer while it was still wet.

This fresco, found in the ruins of the Palace of Knossos, shows people in a game called bull-vaulting. The bull was probably a symbol for the earthquakes that threatened the Minoans' island, and this game might have been a way to pay tribute to the earth's natural forces. It's thought that in the game, an athlete ran very fast toward the bull, grabbed its horns with both hands, and tried to flip over the animal's back and land behind him without getting hurt.

Both men and women participated in the bull-vaulting game. The young women, shown here with light skin, wear bracelets and necklaces and elaborate hair styles. A border painted in a pattern of overlapping stones frames the scene.

ATTRIBUTED TO QASIM IBN ALI. *Shah-nameh: Siyavush Plays Polo Before Afrasiyab*. 1520-40.
Ink, colors, silver and gold on paper, 11 3/16″ x 9 5/16″.
©1992 The Metropolitan Museum of Art, New York. Gift of Arthur A. Houghton, Jr., 1970.(301.26).

Do you think the artist painted this while he was watching
the game? What makes you think that?

There are many fine details in this painting.
Which ones do you find most interesting? Why?

What spot does your eye keep returning to?
Why do you think it does?

If by magic you could become a part of this painting,
where would you choose to be? Explain.

During the rule of the Shah in sixteenth-century Persia, the best artists
were brought to the royal court to illustrate important works of literature.
The richly illustrated manuscripts they produced were among the Shah's
most treasured possessions.

This illustration of a polo game is from a long poem called the *Book of
Kings*. In the painting, Prince Siyavush, who wears a white helmet topped
with several feather plumes, holds his mallet up in the air and is about to
hit the ball. The script above the scene, which continues at the bottom
left, tells us that the prince struck the ball so hard that it flew as high as
the moon. The spectators on the hillside react by blowing horns and beat-
ing drums.

Painting the details in this picture, such as the elaborate decoration on
the clothing and riding tack, required great skill and concentration. The
grouping and placement of the horses and people, the rhythmic repetition
of brilliant colors, and the tufts of grass over the sandy-colored ground
give the painting movement and expression. The horses' arched necks and
prancing legs show the dramatic action of the game.

PIETER BRUEGEL THE ELDER. *Children's Games.* 1560. Oil on wood, 46 ½" x 63 ½".
Kunsthistorisches Museum, Vienna. Photograph © Erich Lessing /Art Resource, New York.

Which of the games in this painting have you played?
Point to them and name them.

Which game looks like the most fun? Why?

Where would you have to be to get this view?

Do you think the artist really saw this scene, or did he make it up?
Explain.

In many of Pieter Bruegel's paintings, groups of people work and play in the midst of panoramic landscapes. These descriptive scenes reveal the artist's careful observation of daily life in northern Europe in the sixteenth century.

In *Children's Games* we see a town populated by children playing more than eighty different games, many of which we can still recognize. Some of the children play leapfrog, ride a hobbyhorse, and roll a hoop. Others play games not so obvious to us today: a group in the center plays dress-up, forming a wedding procession led by two girls carrying a basket. The bride, dressed in dark robes, wears a crown perched atop her head of loosely hanging hair.

Each activity is clearly portrayed against a background of browns and greens. The reds, blues, and blacks in the children's clothing give rhythm and balance to the composition.

KITAGAWA UTAMARO. *Untitled.* Late 1790s. Woodblock, 14 ⁵/₁₆″ x 9 ¹¹/₁₆″.
Bayly Art Museum of the University of Virginia, Charlottesville.

14

Each figure is outlined in black. With your finger, trace the outline, or edge, of the mother's clothes.

What did the artist do to show you that the mother and her children are having a good time?

To make this woodblock print, the artist cut a different block for each color. How many woodblocks do you think were needed for this print?

Though Kitagawa Utamaro was a well-known Japanese artist, no one kept a record of his birthplace, date of birth, or parents, because artists in his time were considered unimportant. One account tells us that Utamaro had an eye for detail when he was very young; he caught fireflies, crickets, and grasshoppers to observe and draw them, then let them go.

Utamaro mastered the art of making woodblock prints, which are noted for their strong lines and vivid, flat colors. To make these, he cut into the surface of a block of hard wood, leaving a raised area to be colored and printed. He placed a piece of paper on the inked surface, then rubbed the paper until the ink was evenly transferred. A different block was needed for each color. By repeating the process, many prints could be made from each set of blocks.

Utamaro portrayed the beauty and pleasure of Japan in his time, often in scenes of daily life. In this print, a mother watches her children play blindman's buff from behind a screen. She wears a flowered robe called a kimono and a wide sash called an obi, which is tied around her waist in a very large bow. One of her children hides behind her clothes, while the other reaches out.

JEAN-SIMÉON CHARDIN. *The House of Cards.* 1741. Oil on canvas, 23 ½″ x 28 ½″.
The National Gallery, London. Reproduced by courtesy of the Trustees.

How does this boy's clothing compare to the way children dress today?

Artists use light to call attention to important parts of their paintings. Point to some places where Chardin used this technique.

In what ways has the artist shown us that this boy is concentrating on what he is doing?

What do you think is in the drawer?

When he was a young man, Jean-Siméon Chardin decided he wanted to become a painter rather than a cabinetmaker like his father. There is a story that while apprenticed in a painter's workshop, he was asked to paint a gun in a portrait. His success in depicting the object encouraged him to focus on still lifes for some time. Later he gained recognition for his scenes of people in everyday activities.

Chardin painted more than one version of *The House of Cards*. For each one, he carefully posed his model and arranged the objects on the table. The boy in this painting, wearing the clothes and hair style that were fashionable in eighteenth-century France, was the son of a cabinetmaker and merchant who was a good friend of the artist. This scene suggests that the boy found playing cards left on the table and decided to make something with them. The cards had been folded after they were used in a game, to prevent someone's cheating by reusing them.

Chardin used soft, harmonious colors in the painting, and made the most of light and shadow to give his subjects depth and shape. The overall effect is one of silence, calm, and order.

GEORGE CATLIN. *Archery of the Mandan*. 1835-37. Oil on canvas, 19 ½" x 27 ⅝".
National Museum of American Art, Washington, D.C. / Art Resource, New York.

Which men seem to be waiting for their turn?
Which men have already played?
Which men are just watching?

Look at the face of the Indian who just shot an arrow.
What does it tell you about how he feels?

Describe the place where the Indians are playing their game.

As a child growing up in Pennsylvania, George Catlin spent many hours hunting, fishing, and looking for American Indian artifacts. His fascination with Native Americans was kindled by his mother, who told him stories of the Western frontier and how she was captured by a tribe when she was a young girl.

Years later, a group of Native Americans came through Philadelphia dressed in their colorful costumes and made quite an impression on Catlin. He decided to leave his law career to paint full-time, and he made up his mind to record the American Indians' way of life before it vanished. For eight years he traveled by steamship, canoe, horse, burro, and on foot to Indian villages. While living with different tribes, he kept a detailed journal and painted their portraits, hunts, rituals, and scenes of domestic life.

In *Archery of the Mandan*, young men compete in a test of skill outside their village on the plains of North Dakota. The archers place treasured articles on the ground as a fee for entering the game, then take turns to see who can get the most arrows flying in the air at one time. Whoever wins gets to take everything home.

WINSLOW HOMER. *Snap the Whip*. 1872. Oil on canvas, 12″ x 20″.
©1992 The Metropolitan Museum of Art, New York. Gift of Christian A. Zabriskie, 1950.(50.41).

Which boy seems to be the leader?
How did the artist show you that?

What other games could you play in a place like this besides snap the whip?

What season does this painting show?
What clues let you know that?

The boys are playing outside their schoolhouse.
Compare this scene to the one outside your school.

Winslow Homer grew up in rural Massachusetts, not far from Boston. He served for a few years as an apprentice to a printmaker, but like many other American artists of his time, he was almost entirely self-taught. Before photographs were widely available, he made on-site sketches of Civil War battlefields for a weekly magazine.

Homer's later work focused mainly on rural life. His paintings vividly recall the outdoor games he played as a child in nineteenth-century rural America. He painted such scenes with a freshness and realism for which he became famous.

In *Snap the Whip*, barefoot boys join hands in a line to run across a field in front of a red schoolhouse. The leader suddenly stops, and the children at the end of the line lose their grip and tumble off. Homer's painting shows his great attention to details that describe the healthy, energetic children, their surroundings, and the effects of weather and light.

MAURICE PRENDERGAST. *The East River*. 1901. Watercolor and pencil on paper, 13 ¾" x 19 ¾".
Collection, The Museum of Modern Art, New York. Gift of Abby Aldrich Rockefeller.

Is this a noisy or quiet place? What makes you think so?

What things in the picture tell you that this is near a large city?

Name as many things as you can find in the painting that were man-made.

This painting is a watercolor. For some areas of the painting, the artist mixed a color, then made it lighter by adding water to it. Find a darker and lighter use of the same color.

At the age of fourteen, Maurice Prendergast left school and took a job wrapping packages in a dry goods store in Boston. In his spare moments he sketched the fabrics and dresses on display and the busy store life around him. His early interest in the colors and patterns in fabric probably influenced his distinctive decorative style.

Prendergast was more interested in color and pattern than in telling a story about life in his time, and the gaily dressed, animated crowds in the public parks of Boston and New York offered perfect subjects for his compositions. Colorful clothing and hats became decorative elements in his scenes.

The transparent effects of watercolor and the artist's placement of colors give his paintings a shimmering quality. The spots of unpainted white paper next to his jewel-like colors also enhance this effect.

In *The East River*, adults and children enjoy a leisurely day in a riverside park in New York City. Subtle brush strokes describe the gesture and pose of each figure. The people look flat, with no shadows or modeling. Most of them have their backs to us, and the few turned toward us have faces without features. People and boats seem equally important in the artist's overall decorative scheme.

HORACE PIPPIN. *Domino Players*. 1943. Oil on composition board, 12 ³/₄″ x 22″.
©The Phillips Collection, Washington, D.C.

What color has the artist used most? Point to the lightest shade of this color. Then find the darkest shade of the same color. How do you think the artist made the darker color?

Find and point to the red areas in the painting. Why do you think the artist used the color red in so many places?

Artists create patterns by repeating shapes or lines. How many different patterns can you find?

Are the domino players having fun? Are they bored? Are they serious? What makes you think so?

When he was a young boy, Horace Pippin won six crayons, a box of watercolors, and two brushes by entering one of his drawings in a magazine contest. Though he had to leave school when he was fourteen to support his sick mother, he continued teaching himself to paint.

Pippin enlisted and served in the U.S. Army in World War I. He kept a diary as a soldier and illustrated it with sketches of the dramatic things he witnessed every day. A bullet paralyzed his right hand during the war, but he continued to paint by using his left hand to guide the hand that held the brush.

Pippin painted *Domino Players* from his memories of childhood, when his family gathered in the kitchen at day's end to play a game of dominoes. A grandmother sits close by and stitches a quilt. The chipping plaster walls, broken window frames, and bare floorboards are clues to the family's poverty.

The dots on the dominoes, the dots on the woman's blouse, and the black-on-red dots on the player's head scarf unite the scene and add interesting detail. The restrained whites, grays, and browns that dominate the painting are enlivened by the red accent areas.

DIEGO RIVERA. *Piñata*. 1953. Tempera on canvas, 97" x 171 ½".
Hospital Infantil de Mexico "Federico Gomez," Mexico City. Reproduced by permission of the hospital.

The children are reacting in different ways to what is happening in this painting. Find a happy child, a sad child, and a frightened child.

Which child looks the most eager to gather the falling fruits and candies? How did the artist show that?

How does the artist show movement in this painting? Describe the different ways.

Where do you think the children are playing? Explain how you decided that.

From the time Diego Rivera could hold a pencil, he drew on walls, doors, and furniture all over the house. To protect the family's property, his father let him have a room in which he could draw wherever he liked.

Rivera's warm earth colors, his flat, decorative style, and clear organization of his subject matter are strongly based in ancient Mexican art. His work tells us about the struggles of the Mexican people, their festivals, and their way of life.

In this painting, a star-shaped clay piñata filled with fruit and candy hangs from a rope just out of reach of some excited children. One blindfolded child hits the piñata with a stick while the other children scramble for the treats.

The breaking of the piñata symbolizes the triumph of good over evil. The fruits and candies, symbolizing good, fall on the participants. At the right, a boy in a blue-and-white poncho is comforted by his mother, who pats him on the head and gives him a piece of Mexican bread called a tortilla.

ELAINE DE KOONING. *Baseball Players*. 1953. Oil on canvas, 17 5/8″ x 23 7/8″.
Telfair Academy of Arts and Sciences, Savannah, Georgia. Gallery Exchange.

What details in this picture tell you that this is a baseball game?
Do you think the player is safe or out?
What in the painting tells you that?

What things in the painting give a sense of noise and action?

Pretend you have a paintbrush in your hand. Select one color in the painting and make the kind of brush strokes you think the artist used to put that color on her canvas. What kind of brush strokes would you use in your own painting of a baseball game?

When Elaine de Kooning was a child, her mother encouraged her interest in art by taking her to museums in New York, providing her with art books, and encouraging her to draw. The walls of their home in Brooklyn were covered with reproductions of famous works of art.

When she was a young artist, the major style of painting in New York was abstract expressionism. As artists used paint to express their feelings and free themselves from old ways of doing things, strong colors and prominent brush strokes became important in their compositions. Sometimes accidental effects appeared in their paintings. Elaine de Kooning's work has roots in this artistic movement.

Throughout her career, the artist worked on several series of paintings on various themes. In the 1950s she produced a series of baseball paintings, each work featuring a different aspect of the game. In *Baseball Players*, two figures dominate the painting. The athletes' power and motion are shown in bold, sketchy brush strokes.

RED GROOMS. *Fast Break*. 1983-84. Painted wood and metal, 48″ x 68 ½″ x 36″.
Private collection, courtesy Marlborough Gallery. ©1992 Red Grooms/ARS, New York.

In what ways did the sculptor make this basketball game look wacky?

Wherever you look in this sculpture, something exciting is happening. Point to two different places and describe what is going on.

Would you like to be in this game? Why or why not?

One of Red Grooms' most vivid childhood memories is of his father making things. His mother, who was very interested in music, was the one who encouraged her son to attend art school. In time, Grooms gained experience as a filmmaker, painter, printmaker, performing artist, and sculptor.

Grooms' work is imaginative, inventive, and full of fun. He reveals his wit and humor through caricature and exaggeration. In *Fast Break*, he combines painting and sculpture to capture an exciting moment in a basketball game. The yellow team has just made a basket, and the coach of the blue team is yelling to his players to hurry to their end of the court to score. The warped look of the floor accentuates the drama of their rough-and-tumble play.

Walking around this sculpture gives the viewer a different perspective of the game's action and the detailed work in the piece. Grooms cut the figures out of pine plank with a jigsaw, painted them, and then secured them to the floor with dowels. Long, flat pieces of wood were used to exaggerate the length of the players' arms and legs. Little pieces of wood were added to form the shoes and socks, and painted shadows and highlights give the figures more dimension.

❖

Look at all the pictures again.

Which games have you played?
Which game looks the most difficult?
Which one looks the quietest?
Which one looks as though it would make the most noise?

When you return to this book another time, you may see things you missed. You may also see the things you saw before in a different way.

KEEP LOOKING!
